NISTIR 7935

FACTS: A Framework for Analysis, Comparison, and Testing of Standards

Paul Witherell
Sudarsan Rachuri
Anantha Narayanan
Jae Hyun Lee
Systems Integration Division
Engineering Laboratory

http://dx.doi.org/10.6028/NIST.IR.7935

May 2013

U.S. Department of Commerce
Rebecca Blank, Acting Secretary

National Institute of Standards and Technology
Patrick D. Gallagher, Under Secretary of Commerce for Standards and Technology and Director

Table of Contents

Abstract: *Open and consensus standards play a critical role in enabling globally-distributed manufacturing. A close connection between standards development and implementation strategies is critical to ensure widespread adoption. Ideally, the development and implementation of standards is based on a clear understanding of information requirements, the modeling of concepts, and different levels of abstraction from multiple stakeholder viewpoints. Towards this goal, we propose a Framework for Analysis, Comparison, and Testing of Standards (FACTS). Based on the Zachman Framework, FACTS-derived information models explicitly model standards from various perspectives and at different levels of abstraction, providing a unified approach for standards development and implementation. In this paper, we explain FACTS and analyze several standards with respect to the different stages of a standard's lifecycle and information modeling abstractions. We outline the role of FACTS in providing implementation and testability strategies for standards. Finally, we explain FACTS using a set of standards in a sustainable manufacturing case study. We envision that FACTS can lead to the development of a CASE-tool-like environment for standards development and implementation.*

Keywords: sustainability standards, Zachman Framework, information modeling, measurement science, knowledge management

1 Motivation: A Case for more Robust Standards

As defined by standards.gov [1], standards are *"the common and repeated use of rules, conditions, guidelines or characteristics for products or related processes and production methods, and related management systems practices."*

The role of standards is to serve as common sets of rules, conditions, guidelines, or characteristics, serving industry, government, and many other stakeholders. Given their widespread application, different organizations have adopted different definitions of standards[1,2], however, their role remains the same. Widely understood as a means for disseminating best practices, over the years standards have evolved and matured to the extent that we unknowingly use them in our daily life. From weights and measures to the modern digital standards, they have become almost omnipresent. For the manufacturing industry, standards can play the important role of defining both products and processes, support interoperability, and promote best practices.

Globalization and increased use of contract manufacturing amplifies the need for manufacturers, suppliers, and service providers to have open, globally acceptable technical standards and the required conformance tests to ensure compatibility. Factors such as globalization have led some to re-evaluate how standards are developed and what constitutes their "success" [2]. Despite their significance, the development and deployment of standards is far from a perfected science. There is lack of uniformity in the ways standards are conceived, developed, implemented, and tested. The inconsistent manners in which standards are developed and deployed can lead to misguided interpretations and ultimately result in ill-defined and ill-implemented standards.

---

[1] http://www.iso.ch
[2] http://standards.ieee.org/develop/overview.html

FACTS, a Framework for Analysis, Comparison, and Testing of Standards, provides a means to analyze, compare, and test a standard. We believe that with additional information formalisms and structure, the way standards are developed, disseminated, and implemented can improve. As such, our approach applies to each stage of a standard's existence, from conceptualization to implementation, and at multiple levels of abstraction, from enterprise level to process level. The result is a standard that will be developed, interpreted, and therefore implemented more consistently and effectively over a wide range of stakeholders.

In this paper, we describe how to utilize information models to address challenges associated with the development and communication of standards. Guided by the Zachman Framework [3], we demonstrate how to develop information models consistently and at various levels of detail. By applying our approach early, developers can identify possible holes in a standard's scope for a given domain of discourse. During implementation, our approach can assist in identifying coverage gaps and overlaps between standard scopes, or at the process level can be used to identify conformance criteria. The flexibility of our application is a result of the framework depending on the development of simple information models and artifacts with the ability to assume contexts from multiple application scenarios.

2 Background: Challenges in the Standard Lifecycle

As with any product, a standard decomposes into individual stages of its lifecycle. The International Electrotechnical Commission (IEC) proposed the standard lifecycle as the following three stages [4]:

1) *Standard Development*- This stage takes a standard from pre-conceptualization and conceptualization to its discussion and finally writing [5]. The stakeholders, represented by producers, distributors, users, consumers, regulators, certifiers, software solution providers, Non-Government Organizations (NGOs) and other interested parties gather within committees and the draft of a standard is prepared.

2) *Standard Deployment/Implementation* - Implementation should occur in a product, service, legislation, or policy or other concrete market-visible offering. Some consortia often first produce a pilot implementation, which is usually a proof of concept study conducted to understand the implementation and ease of adoption issues before an industry-wide implementation.

3) *Standard Renewal/Maintenance*- This stage is reflective of the standard development stage, except there is an existing standard to maintain. At this stage revisions occur.

During the development of a standard, lack of well-defined information structure can lead to insufficiencies when describing the intended domain of discourse. During deployment, lack of well-defined information structure can lead to ambiguities in scope and implementation. This section discusses each of these lifecycle stages, identifies the stakeholders involved at these stages, and addresses how improved information structure can contribute to successful standard execution at each lifecycle stage.

2.1   The Development Stage –Stakeholders: Standard Development Organizations

In manufacturing, standards serve as best and recommended practices to produce quality products and ensure interoperability. With this in mind, it is important to recognize the critical role standards play, and that this role begins with a thorough, collaborative, development process.

Standards are traditionally developed by standards development organizations (SDOs), such as the International Organization for Standardization (ISO), the International Electrotechnical Commission (IEC), and the International Telecommunication Union (ITU); and scientific and engineering societies, such as the American Society for Testing and Materials (ASTM), the American Society for Mechanical Engineers (ASME), the Society of Automotive Engineers (SAE), and the Institute of Electrical and Electronics Engineers (IEEE). Within these organizations are working groups tasked to develop standards to satisfy the specific needs of various stakeholders, each consisting of members who offer both expertise and experience on a subject matter.

Over the years, many independent industry consortia and NGOs have sprung up and have fast tracked standards development processes. This is largely due to increased demand for standards in specific domains. In these cases, more than any, standards must satisfy the needs of a particular set of stakeholders, irrespective of the fact that similar standards may already exist for the domain of interest. For a more thorough analysis of standards development processes, as well as economics, politics, and legal reviews, one can refer to works by Cargill [5], Egyedi [6], Krislov [7], and Kahin [8].

Regardless of whether the consortia represent the needs of the many (SDOs) or the few (independent efforts), significant obstacles must often be overcome before parties reach an agreement on documentation and content. Solutions often involve expanding content to reach necessary compromises, leading to bloated standards. By placing priorities on content and the quantity of knowledge represented, communication needs are often overlooked. As a result, the quality of a standard's representation can adversely affect all aspects of a standard's lifecycle.

An objective analysis of the problem domain is necessary to address developmental challenges effectively. With clear boundaries and the ability to deconstruct a domain, goals that are more concise can be put forth. The ability to define more concise goals inevitably leads to better articulation and therefore more explicit information requirements within the standard.

2.2   The Deployment/Implementation Stage - Stakeholders: Industry, Software Solution Providers, Government, Consumers

The first step of standards deployment is identifying the appropriate standard, or often standards to adopt. This is not often an easy task, as standards and regulations may differ at many levels, across trading regions, as well as industry sectors. Variety can create substantial issues for implementation and promotion of standards, increasing the cost of doing business.

The second and third steps of standards deployment are conformance and compliance. Conformance necessitates identifying the information requirements for a standard's implementation. For industry, conformance may influence what data is important to capture and

3

track during the development of a product. However, structural conformance to a standard does not imply operational compliance with the standard [9]. Operational compliance requires that industry has verified, usually through a government or certification agency, that their product satisfies any operational criteria set forth in the standard. In each case, well-defined, explicit requirements are necessary to determine whether criteria are satisfied.

A primary challenge faced during standard deployment is converting the knowledge of the domain experts into usable information for respective stakeholders. Explicit information models alleviate this challenge by providing structured information where conformance and compliance criteria are easily recognized. By explicitly identifying the information requirements of standards an enterprise can 1) associate standard requirements with products and product data, 2) align its proprietary information management techniques with the information requirements of standards, and 3) compare and contrast requirements from multiple standards to understand differences in conformance criteria and product coverage [10].

2.3 The Renewal/Maintenance Stage – Stakeholders: Standards Developers, Standards Implementers

Standard renewal/maintenance is very similar to the standards development process, and therefore faces many of the same issues. The renewal/maintenance stage addresses the updating and refinement of standards. At this stage, unlike with the development process, a consortium previously achieved a consensus, and there is existing documentation. Our methodology allows standards developers to take a structured approach when revisiting their initial development efforts and reduce the possibility of "bloating" the standard with redundant or unproductive information requirements.

The authors believe the primary challenges presented by current standardization processes are as follows: 1) current standards are not formalized enough or well supported through an information technology infrastructure; 2) individual standards can vary greatly, in both detail and scope, even when sharing a single intent; and 3) improved mechanisms are needed for testing, conformance, and branding processes to ensure the compliance of products to standardized specifications. Each of these challenges can be addressed, at least partially, by improved structure and formalisms in the standard development, deployment, and maintenance processes. In the next section, we discuss previous efforts on adding structure at both the macro (groups of standards) and micro (individual standards) levels of standard organization.

3 Literature Review: The Classification and Comparison of Standards

Previous research efforts have led to some formalization of standards and standard content, at both the macro and micro level. Here, we review the motivations behind these formalizations and discuss some of the results.

Macro-level classifications can help stakeholders identify with and analyze against pre-existing standards for a given domain. At the development stage, these classifications can help SDOs address insufficiencies between a standard's scope and intent. At the maintenance stage, macro-level classifications can help stakeholders manage the information requirements from a family of standards. In general, macro-level classifications can facilitate the harmonization of standards by providing insight into information requirements of similar standards.

There are many research efforts for comparing and harmonizing standards. Many of the macro-level efforts for standard classification have come in support of Product Lifecycle Management (PLM)[11-14]. Beyond PLM efforts, Sudarsan et al. [15], proposed a hierarchical typology of standards to reflect the content to be communicated and imply the appropriate expressiveness and language choices for each type. In [16], the authors sketched a method towards comparing and harmonizing information standards based on: 1) informal approach, 2) typology of standards, 3) use-case scenarios, and 4) ontologies. Panetto et al. [17] proposed a mapping of IEC 62264 [18] standard models onto the Zachman framework. The paper explains how to exploit the recursiveness of the Zachman framework to deal with different views of stakeholders. In [19], the authors use 36 different characterizations to classify healthcare and healthcare information system standards based on informatics.

In the healthcare industry, The Healthcare Information Technology Standards Panel [20] (HITSP) was formed to promote and facilitate the harmonization of standards used to exchange health data in the United States. As part of this effort, HITSP addressed various challenges of the standards, especially gaps, overlaps, and missing coverage. Their efforts took the classification of standards one step further, formally defining a set of terminology for comparison.

The HITSP has defined the following terms with respect to a standard:

- Harmonization – the selection of standards most appropriate to support specific events, actions, and actors in a use case.
- Context – the unique requirements of a specific actor within a use case.
- Gap – missing or incomplete standards that are required to support events in a use case.
- Overlap – overlaps refer to instances where some or all of the requirements are met by multiple standards.

We have incorporated this terminology into our work, and these definitions highlight where much of our early efforts have focused.

Earlier efforts in macro-level analyses tested our methodology using comparisons within a family of sustainability-related standards. In [21] gaps and overlaps of select standards were studied as they pertained to stages of a product's lifecycle. The gaps and overlaps were used to identify with a specific standard and the lifecycle phases of products to which it applied.

To classify standards at the macro, or family, level there must be some understanding of the standard at the micro, or individual level. While most standard formalization efforts have come at the macro-level (standard classification), we propose any true synthesis of standards requires formalizations at both the macro and micro (information models for a single standard) levels.

4 Framework for the Formalization of Content

Our work at NIST has explored enterprise architecture frameworks as a means to bridge the perceived gap between standards as developed by domain experts and those standards as understood by stakeholders. Our approach, FACTS, is partially based on the Zachman

Framework. In this section, we discuss how the Zachman Framework acts as the foundation of our FACTS approach. We explain how the framework's fundamentals can assist in the development of a more elaborate analysis, comparison, and testing environment for standards.

4.1   Introduction to the Zachman Framework

The Zachman Framework was originally developed by John Zachman for enterprise architecture design [22]. The Zachman Framework for enterprise architecture consists of a two dimensional, 6 x 6 matrix, as shown in Figure 1. The meanings of the phrases in the cells in Figure 1 become clear as we describe an example later. The columns of the framework are formed by the six cognitive primitives [23]: What, How, When, Who, Where, and Why. Each question primitive represents an aspect of information: 'What' is concerned with data, 'How' with process or function, 'When' with time cycle related information, 'Who' with information about people and organizations, 'Where' with geographical locations, and 'Why' is concerned with enterprise level motivations and goals. The rows represent different perspectives. The upper rows represent high-level views of the enterprise, while the lower rows generally represent views that require additional detail.

	What (Data)	How (Function)	When (Time)	Who (People)	Where (Location)	Why (Motivation)
Scope (Contextual)	List of things	List of processes	List of events	List of organizations	List of locations	List of goals
Enterprise Model (Conceptual)	Semantic model	Business process model	Master schedule	Work flow model	Logistics network	Business plan
System Model (Logical)	Logical data model	Application architecture	Processing structure	Human interface architecture	Distributed system architecture	Business rule model
Technology Model (Physical)	Physical data model	System design	Control structure	Presentation architecture	Technology architecture	Rule design
Implementation (Detail)	Data definition	Programs	Timing definition	Security architecture	Network architecture	Rule specification
Functioning Enterprise	Usable data	Working function	Usable network	Functioning organization	Implemented schedule	Working strategy

Figure 1: The Zachman Framework

Each cell of the matrix models a discrete portion of the enterprise. For example, the cell at the intersection of the 'how' column and the 'System Model' perspective models the designer's view of the system's function. Zachman calls this model the system architecture model. After all the cell models have been constructed, they can be integrated to realize an enterprise as a whole.

4.2   Leveraging the Zachman Framework

Despite being an enterprise architecture framework, it is important to recognize that different interpretations can exist for the Zachman rows and columns. While the cells of the Zachman framework provide a clear decomposition of the enterprise, there are no restrictions on the specific models or notations allowed in each of the cells. In general, the Zachman Framework helps decompose and analyze any system that is complex to understand.

The Zachman framework provides a holistic view of any system while maintaining tractability through the careful separation of concerns. The value of any methodology based on this framework lies in the dimensions in which the problem can be decomposed. The separation provided by the cognitive primitives and layers of abstraction allow us to break down an idea into orthogonal dimensions. This separation also provides a means for reconstructing desired idea segments from different cells by integrating the rows and the columns of the framework. This framework approach allows stakeholders to analytically define and reason about various disparate issues encountered when coping with standards.

5 Methodology: FACTS

Standards analysis in the FACTS methodology results in explicit, deliberate information models in the columns and rows of the Zachman framework. A standard's scope can be explicitly represented at the contextual level by identifying, through lists, its individual traits. These traits provide concise answers to the 'What,' 'How,' 'When,' "Who,' 'Where,' and 'Why' questions. After establishing a domain of discourse, the topmost rows can help identify the important high-level concepts and their relationships within a standard. The middle rows provide the logical and physical models to specific stakeholders to represent the logical and physical details associated with standard implementation. Finally, the lowest rows describe the implementation.

This section explains the FACTS approach: the analysis processes, how to compare two different standards, and how to test for conformance and consistency of a standard based on analyzed models.

5.1   Analysis and Modeling of a Standard's Domain

The analysis of a standard using the FACTS methodology consists of a stakeholder analysis and a technical analysis. The stakeholder analysis provides understanding of a standard from different stakeholders' perspectives, and the technical analysis provides explicit, analyzed models of the standard using the Zachman framework.

5.1.1   Stakeholder Analysis

When developing a methodology to holistically analyze a standard, it is important to consider the needs of different stakeholders and their perspectives, and these considerations are made with our stakeholder analysis. Stakeholders may vary by organization, such as industry, SDOs, NGOs, or government, or across enterprises, such as management, supervisors, or workers. We have developed the following list of stakeholders, based on different perspectives from which one might view a standard: 1) generic user, 2) consumer or buyer, 3) manufacturer or producer, 4) government or regulatory agency, 5) software solution provider, 6) researcher, and 7) standards developer. Each stakeholder may also have multiple perspectives. For example, a manufacturing company can be either a buyer or a producer, depending on whether it uses a standard for manufacturing a product or for purchasing supplied parts.

Viewing a standard from different perspectives is necessary because each perspective may raise unique issues, or concerns, on the extent to which a standard addresses a perspective's requirements. For instance, if we consider the primitive 'how', a consumer or buyer is mainly interested in: "How to verify that a product is standard compliant?" A manufacturer or producer may ask a question such as, "How do I become compliant and obtain certification?" A government agency may be interested in how to regulate a standard or how to promote it. A software solution provider may be interested in data availability or possible implementability and scalability issues of the standard. A researcher may be interested in how to obtain statistics for a standard's evaluation. A standards developer may be interested in how to provide implementation training. Different concerns such as these illustrate the need to analyze standards from the perspectives of all the stakeholders involved.

Our stakeholder analysis is comprised of the following steps: 1) selecting a standard, 2) identifying sets of concerns from each stakeholder perspective based on the question primitives of the Zachman framework, 3) and positioning the concerns in appropriate cells of the Zachman framework. The stakeholder analysis gathers requirements and provides general observations of what a detailed technical analysis may entail. At the development stage of a standard, the stakeholder analysis helps to assess the stakeholder needs when assessing the standards' requirements and scope. Stakeholder analysis at the deployment stage allows stakeholders to assess a standard within the scope of his/her particular needs.

Once the stakeholder analysis has been finalized, we must complete the transition from the stakeholder analysis to the technical analysis. Each stakeholder's concern may relate to one or more different cells in the Zachman framework. The mapping of concerns from the stakeholder to the technical analysis influences the technical results and, therefore, should be carefully considered before beginning the technical analysis. Different information models, providing various levels of understanding, are created depending on where the concerns are positioned in the matrix. We expand upon this idea in Section 6.1.2.

5.1.2 Technical Analysis

The stakeholder analysis provides insight into the entities associated with a standard, such as the actors, processes, products, or materials. The technical analysis aspect of FACTS models these entities so they can be easily interpreted and their roles understood by all. As Zachman provides an enterprise modeling approach, we discuss the analysis results in terms of an appropriate information model for a particular cell.

When analyzing a domain with the Zachman framework, each cell of the 6x6 matrix facilitates an extensive analysis for its designated subset of the problem. The development of the information model for each cell is guided by the cell's meta-model. The meta-models defined in the Zachman Framework provide guidance for how to represent the analysis results at each cell. Figure 2 shows the meta-model for the second row of 'what' column and an information model example of the relationship between a material and a product.

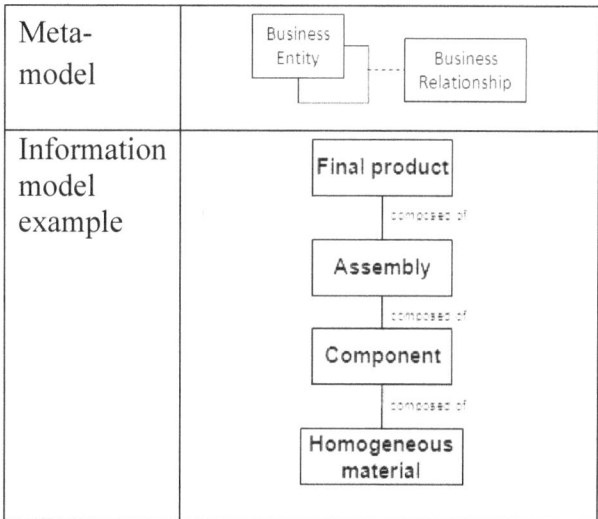

Figure 2. Meta-model and information model example

Once models have been developed for individual cells, each cell model can be related to other models in the same column as well as in the same row. The integration of all cell models in one row constitutes an aggregate model from the perspective of that row. These inter-row relationships promote the continuity of the levels of abstraction between columns. For instance, consider the statement "Standard A applies to manufacturers when participating in Process B in Geographical Location C." In this statement, the 'who,' 'what', 'where,' 'when,' and 'how' can be tied together as they relate to a product, giving insight into Standard A's application. In the following paragraphs we discuss the knowledge gained from each level of abstraction and the methods used to model this knowledge. Further details can be found in [24], and additional models can be found in appendix. In Section 6 we also provide more concrete examples and additional detail in a case study.

Rows 1 and 2: Domain of Discourse. The top two rows of the Zachman Framework serve to establish the domain of discourse, or scope. They identify the main goals of the standard, the most important concepts in the domain, the high-level processes in the domain, and the people and organizations responsible for various activities. Zachman recommends that the cells in the first row, called the contextual row, are simple lists of words. For instance, the first row of the 'what' column will contain important concepts in the standard as a list of nouns. These concepts may also reside in other columns. The second row, called the conceptual row, is a basic entity-relationship model that provides the enterprise model for standard implementation decision making and planning. For instance, the second row of the 'what' column will contain the conceptual object model that identifies the semantic relationships between the concepts identified in the first row.

The analyses results from upper-row abstractions provide stakeholders with the information necessary to make high-level decisions, such as deciding which products should meet a standard or identifying in which countries a standard applies. Our application of the Zachman framework at the upper levels creates generic models and extensive reference data that can be leveraged in further analyses at lower rows, or levels, of abstraction.

9

Rows 3 and 4: Design Interest. The third and fourth rows of the framework contain the "logical" and "physical" abstractions for different stakeholder perspectives of a standard. We use these rows to develop the technical models that support the stakeholder implementation of a standard. The models in these rows contain technical design information at a finer level of detail, but not the complete implementation details. For instance, the third row analysis of the 'what' column will provide logical data models (See [24] for detailed example). These models use the data items defined in the first row of the 'what' column, along with the relationships defined in the second row (semantic model). The fourth row of the 'what' column will contain the physical data model. We consider this model as a specialization of the third row, or an instantiation of the model's structure. It forms the basis for the data definition in the fifth row.

Rows 5 and 6: Implementation Interest. The fifth row of the framework contains the detailed models required for the implementation of the system. For instance, the fifth row of the 'what' column will contain a data definition model, such as database definitions, and will be derived from the model in the fourth row of the 'what' column. The sixth row does not contain any models, but represents the working system itself. These last two rows of the framework are required to realize the implementation of the stakeholder's interest in the standard.

5.2   Comparison of Standards

Following the analysis portion of the FACTS methodology is standard comparison. The comparison aspect of the methodology allows for the identification of gaps and overlaps between two or more analyses results. Top row comparisons will compare scopes, and can help in scenarios such as selecting the right standard for a product. Comparisons at the lower levels of abstraction can help address the complexities of implementing multiple standards. The following sections discuss in detail how comparisons can provide valuable knowledge about standard usage from both general and stakeholder-oriented perspectives.

5.2.1   Rows 1 and 2 Comparison

Comparison at the high levels of abstraction can help identify shared roles and activities of different standards, as well as the distinct differences between them. The overlaps at the top rows of the framework can help synthesize a family of standards based on scopes and enterprise models. High-level gaps can help identify areas where the coverage of a standard scope is lacking or non-existent. At the higher levels of abstraction, we identify two types of gaps and overlaps: 1) those from comparing the same scopes at different levels of detail, and 2) those from comparing similar standards where the scope of one extends beyond the other.

As noted by HITSP [20], similar standards offering different levels of detail can create gaps in coverage. In this scenario, a gap and overlap may exist at the same time. For instance, two standards may overlap in scope; however, the specifics of the scope's coverage may create gaps. These gaps and overlaps often occur when different standards bodies develop similar standards that address the same domain. As different stakeholders have different needs, the result is standards that emphasize details in different places.

When gaps are a result of the extent to which a domain is covered, variations may be driven by factors such as on a specific product type or geographical location. For instance, one standard may cover "desktop computers" while another may cover "computers," therefore extending coverage to notebook computers as well. Here, divergence between standards helps interested parties understand the specifics of when one standard may apply over another.

Analyses and comparison results at the highest levels of abstraction are, for the most part, stakeholder-independent; however, the impact of these comparisons will depend on the stakeholder's perspective. For instance, from an SDO's perspective, comparisons can help place a focus on individual areas in a domain where a new standard may be required or additional detail is needed. For manufacturers and software developers, comparisons may help identify where information gathering and management techniques should be concentrated. For manufacturers, in certain scenarios, this may also mean indirectly conforming to one standard based on the direct conformance to another.

At the lower levels of abstraction, the comparisons become more logical and physical based. Here, the advantage of the gaps and overlaps comparison becomes less focused on when a standard may or may not apply, but how a standard may be implemented.

5.2.2   Rows 3 to 6 Comparison

As noted above, comparisons of standards at the lower rows of abstraction carry different meaning than those at higher levels of abstraction. While the higher levels of abstraction offer the ability to reflect on the "bigger picture" of standard implementation, comparisons at the lower levels can model stakeholder-specific details of implementation. These comparisons include the comparison of logical models, physical models, and detailed models.

When comparing results at the lower levels of abstraction, it is useful to combine individual cells of the analyses as "sentences," having both subjects and predicates. These sentences can provide executable instructions. For instance, at the third level of abstraction, gaps are likely to be a result of differences in implementation requirements. By stringing together "sentences," the manufacturer can develop instructions for implementing different standards, including who is responsible for executing these procedures. Further benefits result when comparing the technology-constrained (physical) and implementation (detail) models located in the two bottom rows. At these levels of abstraction, gaps may result from different machines or even different software.

The main advantages offered by comparisons at the lower levels of abstraction are to provide implementation-centric views and provide insight into how to streamline and simplify implementation practices. At this level, a manufacturer can determine what procedures need to be in place to conform to a particular standard given variances in products, processes, and markets.

5.3   Testing of Standards

The third portion of the FACTS methodology is testing. There are two primary phases to testing standards. One phase, verification testing, (development/maintenance stages) tests for whether the standard itself is sound, i.e., does the standard capture all the requirements that it was designed for, and is it practical to implement. The other phase, validation testing, (deployment) tests for whether a product or process meets the structural and operational requirements of the standard, which is also called conformance testing or conformity assessment. We describe these two phases of standards testing in the subsections below.

5.3.1 Test for standard scope and consistency

Testing for scope and consistency addresses how well a standard addresses its intended scope, and is primarily applied during the standard's development and maintenance stages. The FACTS methodology enables one to: 1) evaluate the intended coverage of a standard's scope, 2) determine whether the standard's high-level goals are aligned and consistent with the information content of the standard, and 3) determine whether a conformance assessment will lead to fulfilling the high-level goals of the standard.

Testing for coverage of scope begins by understanding the standards intent, and its application to various perspectives. Consistency checks can be executed by testing whether the low-level information models satisfy the high-level goals of the standards. Testing for consistency begins by tracing whether the logical and physical models in each column correctly lead to the contextual and conceptual bases in the top rows of the framework. The separation of concerns along the two dimensions offered by the Zachman framework allows us to individually analyze various aspects of the standard, so that we objectively test for congruence between the standard's high-level goals and its logical, physical, and detailed models.

5.3.2 Test for standard conformance

Conformance testing is applied at the standard deployment stage and is used to test for both structural and operational requirements. Conformance testing helps ensure that a standard plays a useful role in promoting quality and reliable products in the market, and minimizes the number of defective or unsuitable products reaching the shelves. The ISO/IEC 17000[25] vocabulary defines "conformity assessment" as "the demonstration that specified requirements relating to a product, process, system, person, or body are fulfilled." Conformity assessment falls under three categories, depending on who performs the assessment: first party assessment, or self-certification, is performed by the seller or manufacturer of a product; second party assessment is performed by the purchaser or user; and third party assessment is performed by an independent entity that has no interest in the transaction between the first and second parties.

The results from the FACTS analysis provide the appropriate information models to assist in evaluating for product conformity. FACTS may be used to explicitly identify and address declaration requirements. When testing for conformance, FACTS may help streamline processes to meet testing criteria prior to conformance testing. Once all requirements have been identified, analyses results from our FACTS approach can then help determine and implement a conformance assessment strategy.

At the conceptual and contextual layers of the framework, conformance testing can help determine the impact of non-conformance. For example, an examination of the top rows of the technical analysis for a standard may reveal that non-conformity would keep a product from participating in a particular market. If the risks associated with non-conformance are quite high, conformance becomes a necessity. Once the need and scope for conformance have been decided, a plan must be set up to perform the conformance assessment.

Utilizing analyses results from lower rows of the technical analysis, comprehensive plans can be devised to test and maintain standard compliance. The lower level rows of the Zachman framework contain the physical and implementation models able to capture the complexities of information associated with a product. These models help determine what type of information should be included in declarations, such as assemblies, solderable parts, and manufacturing process information. This information can then be mapped back to the top rows of abstraction, to ensure that the conformance testing and declaration are aligned with the high-level goals of the standard.

Beyond conformance planning, our framework also helps in developing computable information models to test for conformance. When appropriate, a 'test suite' can be developed similar to test suites in software testing. The models for conformance testing will identify the specific inputs, test methods, and required outputs for testing conformance. The models used will align with the six columns of the Zachman framework.

The FACTS methodology is useful not only in the technical analysis of standards, but also helps to develop a comprehensive coverage through validation testing and a conformance testing framework, which will play a crucial role in industry adoption of the standard. The next section discusses the application of FACTS in a proof-of-concept scenario.

6 FACTS Test-Case

A recent, global example of the challenges that can be created by standards was with the introduction of RoHS [26] (Restriction of Hazardous Substances Directive) by the European Union. Ill-prepared manufacturers were forced to implement ad hoc solutions to support compliance. There was no coordinated effort to create a process that would ensure compliance. Had additional structure been in place, many of the challenges may have been better received and handled.

In 2006, when the RoHS regulation was enforced by the European Union, industry was not fully prepared, but still forced to react due to the regulatory nature of the standard. Manufacturers needed methods to demonstrate that their products (including their supply chain) met the guidelines set forth by RoHS to sell on the European market. This required explicit declarations of information requirements that were inexplicitly defined.

In addressing the challenges presented by RoHS, one of the more widely adopted solutions came in the form of IPC-1752 [27]. Many implementers turned to a NIST-developed information model for the standard [28], along with a prototype tool called SCRIBA [29] for implementation. Our framework and methodology hope to replicate success stories such as these by providing, for any standard, explicit, repeatable formalisms and sound information models.

In this section, we illustrate the application of FACTS, in detail, by applying it to an implementation of the RoHS regulation. We also discuss other standards, such as IPC-1752, to provide a more complete example for FACTS analyses, comparisons, and testing.

6.1 Example: RoHS

The FACTS proof-of-concept implementation of RoHS begins with the stakeholder analysis and continues to the technical analysis.

6.1.1 Analyzing the requirements of various stakeholders

Surveys, workshops, and reference materials are all means for identifying concerns and issues for a RoHS stakeholder analysis. Figure 3 illustrates possible concerns for a generic user, consumer or buyer, and manufacturer or producer (based on Sustainability Standards Portal [30]). The 'v' symbol shows where in the Zachman framework each concern is positioned. This preliminary positioning is necessary for transitioning from the stakeholder analysis to the technical analysis. Guidelines for placement were given in 5.2. In Figure 3, it can be seen that in our scenario most concerns revolved around high-level abstractions.

Selected Standard Name		RoHS					
Stakeholder	ID	Concerns	Contextual	Conceptual	Logical	Technology	Detail
Generic User	Q001	What is this standard/directive?	v				
	Q002	Why RoHS restricts the use of these six substances?	v				
	Q003	Why was this standard/directive developed?	v	v			
Consumer/buyer	Q004	Why is this standard important?		v	v		
	Q005	How to verify and ensure that a product is compliant to this standard?	v				
	Q006	What is this standard about?	v				
Industry/Provider	Q007	Why I should follow this standard?	v	v			
	Q008	How to get certified?		v			

Figure 3. Stakeholder's concerns example.

When identifying stakeholder concerns with RoHS, one noteworthy finding is that the RoHS document does not provide instructions on how to implement RoHS in industry practice. RoHS instead focuses on how to regulate restricted materials in a product that is sold in the European market, leaving implementation concerns unaddressed. Most concerns about the logical, physical, and detailed models had to be addressed with the development of IPC-1752. Therefore, the IPC-1752 standard also serves as a reference.

6.1.2 Technical analysis using Zachman Framework

To transition to the technical analysis for these high-level concerns, we initially concentrate on those cells in the first row used to analyze the contextual aspect, or scope, of RoHS. Figure 4 illustrates how the concerns from individual stakeholders, and the stakeholder analysis, provide a foundation for the technical analysis. Different stakeholders' concerns are transitioned to a set of terms and concepts that provide the basis for establishing the domain of discourse for individual columns. The remainder of this section will discuss the technical analyses that followed this transition.

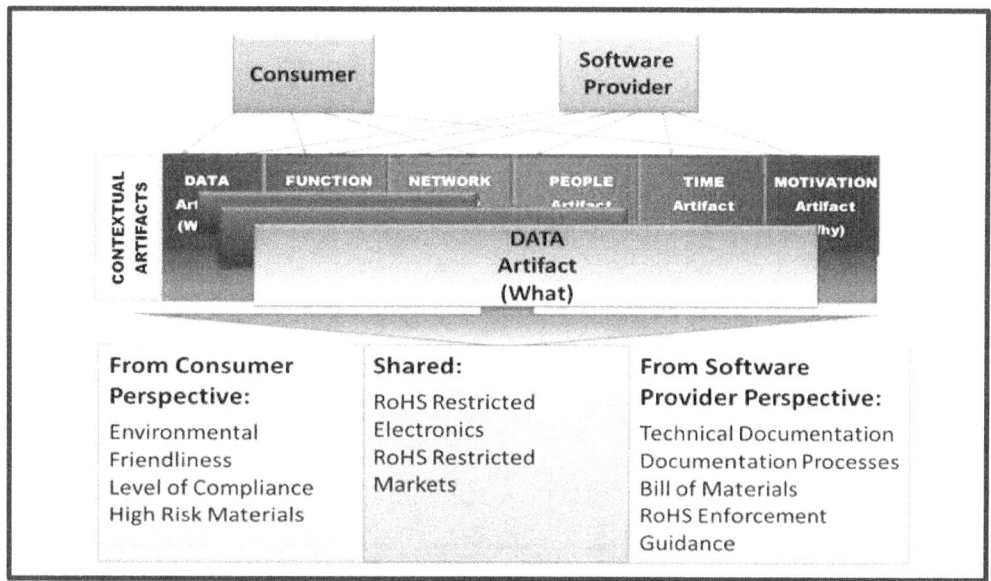

Figure 4. Transition to contextual level of technical analysis

To conduct a technical analysis of the contextual row, we will begin with the 'What' column. In first defining 'What', we consider only physical entities associated with RoHS, such as the materials, products, and information involved. When identifying 'How', we adopt the Supply-Chain Operations Reference (SCOR) [6] model and identify the source, make, and deliver processes of the supply chain as processes impacted by RoHS. The 'Where' aspect of Zachman identifies geographical areas where RoHS is active. The 'Who' aspect identifies the parties or organizations to which RoHS is critical. Parties identified include electronics manufacturers and suppliers, government agencies, and customers. The 'When' row identifies events that initiate process cycles. At the most abstract level, we defined these events as the buying and selling of electronic goods. The 'Why' identifies the high-level goals of RoHS, namely to reduce environmental contamination or to improve brand image. Note that in defining the scope we were careful not to narrow the scope to a point where the RoHS application becomes ill-defined and perspectives are overlooked, yet not broaden the scope to a point where the analysis loses its effectiveness. Figure 5 shows an example of how entities defined in different columns at the first row can be associated to create context and scope.

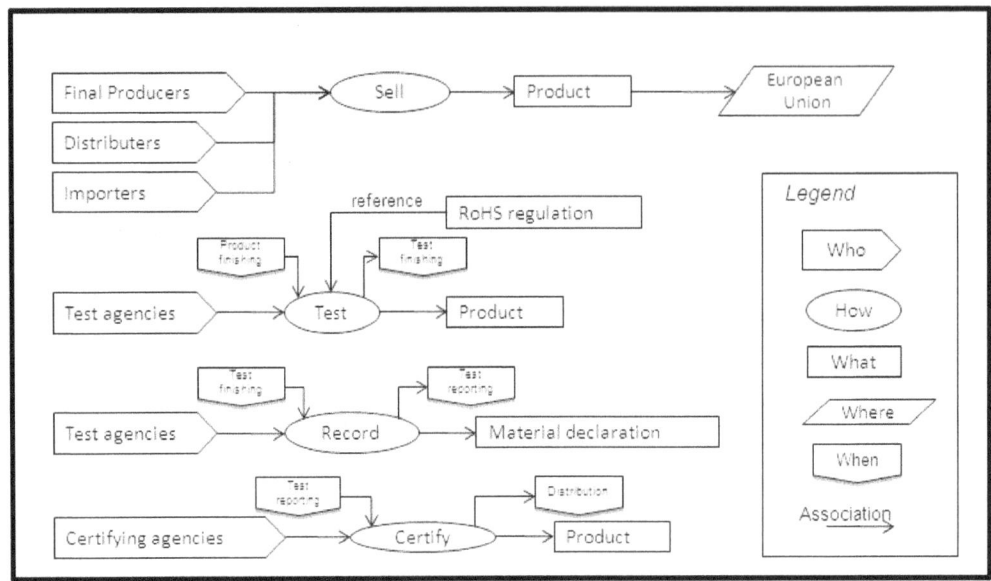

Figure 5. RoHS example of the first row integration.

As the technical analysis progresses from row to row, we will focus on the 'what' column to address changes in levels of abstraction. At the contextual level, the 'what' column provided the "list of things" associated with RoHS. The second row, or the conceptual row, now defines a business, or "semantic" model for RoHS. Using the "list of things" provided in row one, a "business entity-business relationship" model is derived. This model provides details on how entities associated with RoHS interact. For instance, an "assembly" is "composed of" a "component," which is "composed of" a "homogenous material" (See Figure 2). Unlike the lists created in row 1, in row 2 the business models may differ based on the stakeholder perspective taken.

Progressing downward in the 6x6 matrix, the third row provides the logical data model. Logical models are where data entities and their relationships exist. For instance, here a stakeholder may find an information model, including attributes, of a "homogenous material." The fourth row contains the Physical Data model. This model is technology constrained. Therefore, where the logical model provided the attributes of a "homogenous material," the physical data model describes how it is defined, and may vary depending on syntax used. Finally, the fifth row, or the detailed row, contains the data definition. While row 4 describes how a homogenous material is to be defined, row 5 provides its definition. For instance, row 5 may contain a definition detailing the composition of a particular solder in an electronic product.

This section provided detailed insight into how one might analyze RoHS using FACTS. The next session will discuss how analysis results can be used in standard comparison.

6.2   Comparison of RoHS with other Sustainability Standards

In Section 6.2, we discuss the comparison portion of FACTS. Here, we present a proof-of-concept gaps and overlaps comparison between three different standards: 1) RoHS, 2) WEEE (Waste Electrical and Electronics Equipment Directive) [31], and 3) IEEE (Institute of Electrical and Electronics Engineers) P1680 [32]. Each of these standards supports or regulates the sustainability of electronics products. To stay aligned with the original stakeholder concerns and analysis results, here we focus on comparisons at the contextual level of abstraction to understand the gaps and overlaps of the scope of three standards.

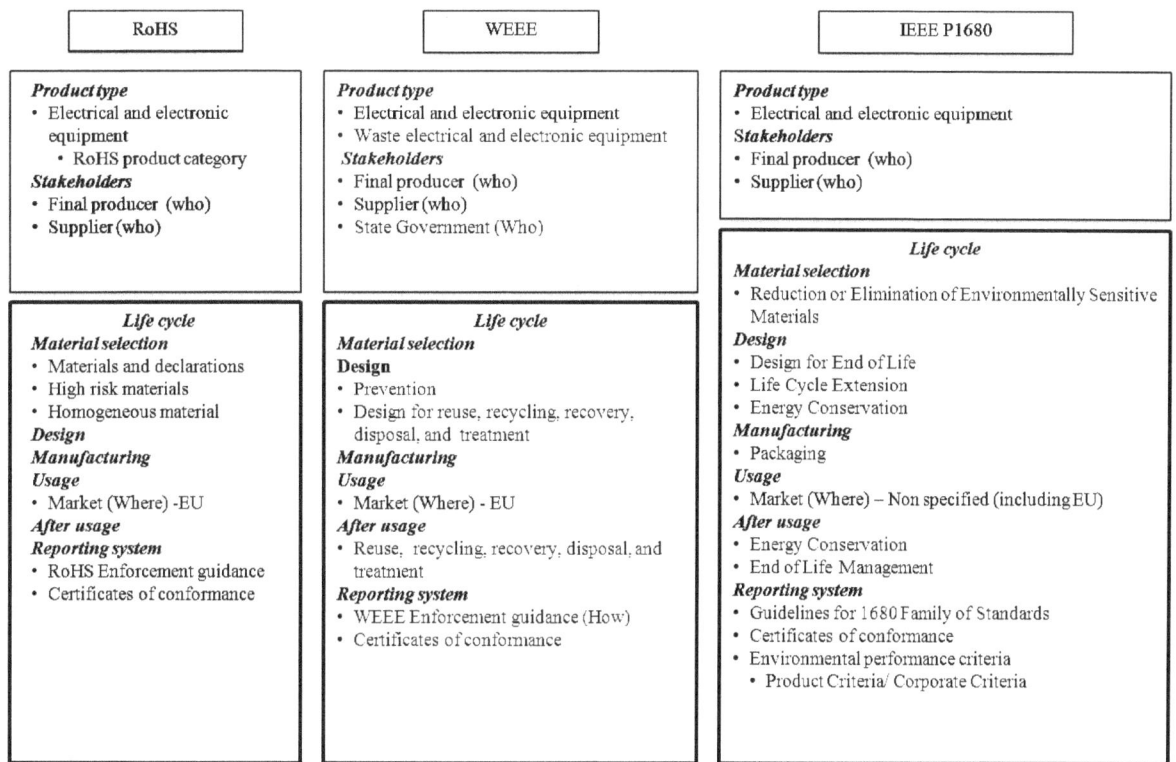

Figure 6. Comparison of standards.

Prior to performing the gaps and overlaps comparison, contextual analyses had to be completed for WEEE and IEEE P1680. Three separate tables (Figure 6) were created from the results of the contextual analyses; each table has a list of words that define the scope of the standard. Gaps and overlaps between coverage can be identified when comparing the three tables within Figure 6.

The specific type of electronics addressed varies between each standard. WEEE encompasses all electronics, while RoHS addresses only ten specific product categories. The P1680 standard serves as a general electronic standard for other standards, limiting specifics. Complementary standards developed to utilize P1680 currently include standards for computers, imaging equipment, and televisions. This variation raises the following issues with standard comparisons: 1) the need to differentiate between the level of detail (as it pertains to standards) and the level of abstraction (as it pertains to Zachman) and 2) the need to address the existence of directly- and indirectly-stated information as it pertains to standards. For this proof-of-concept, we will focus on only what is stated directly in the documents.

In relation to 1), above, recall the discussion in Section 5 of how a Zachman-based analysis offers different levels of abstraction, and how additional details are learned from each level of abstraction. Some standards are more comprehensive than others, leaving gaps in the level of detail. This can be seen between RoHS, WEEE and P1680. WEEE and P1680 aim to address "environmentally sensitive" materials, while RoHS identifies six specific substances. In comparison is it important to identify when gaps are a result of variances in scope, and when they are simply a result of variances in detail. From a manufacture's viewpoint, differences in scope will dictate which of the three standards a product should conform to, while differences in detail will drive the granularity of product information that must be managed. For instance, RoHS focuses on the manufacturing stage of the product, while both WEEE and P1680 address multiple stages of a product lifecycle.

The most important thing learned from this comparison was how each standard affected the manufacture's ability to participate in the European market. In the comparison of the 'why' column, the motivation for compliance of P1680 was determined to be the reduction of environmental impact, improvement of brand image, and achievement of market recognition through different levels of compliance. All of these reasons were to provide voluntary motivation, and left to the manufacturer to decide if compliance is worth the cost. RoHS and WEEE, however, were developed as directives. As European Union (EU) directives, compliance is no longer voluntary. In order for the manufacturer to sell its product in the EU, it must comply with both RoHS and WEEE.

Now that we have discussed a proof-of-concept comparison, in the following section we discuss testing for conformance. Here we will use RoHS and IPC-1752 as an example.

6.3   Testing for conformance and compliance

The stated goals of RoHS are to restrict the presence of substances that are hazardous to the environment and to human health. An examination of the top rows of the Zachman analysis for RoHS reveals that non-conformity would lead to the product being ineligible for the European market. To understand the conformance testing aspect of the FACTS framework, let us consider the RoHS regulation and the IPC-1752 standard. In this section, we use the FACTS framework to determine a conformance strategy for the IPC-1752 standard and provide a detailed plan from start to finish.

IPC-1752 is used for tracking materials declaration between suppliers and Original Equipment Manufacturers (OEMs). As such, OEMs are responsible for not only what they produce, but also what is purchased from suppliers. As a means to satisfy RoHS requirements explicitly, IPC-1752 provides the following four classes of materials declaration:

1. *Class A query/response*: supplier provides true/false responses to predetermined compliance statements
2. *Class B material group*: supplier provides total mass for each "material group"
3. *Class C product level*: supplier provides mass of substances when above threshold level (includes RoHS substances)
4. *Class D homogeneous material*: supplier lists homogeneous materials in product and provides mass of substances for each homogeneous material

These explicit classes address entities very similar to those seen in the results of the earlier analysis of RoHS. IPC-1752 has special RoHS queries for declaring whether a product meets RoHS requirements completely, does not meet RoHS requirements, or falls under a selected exemption. It also allows for capturing detailed information at the homogenous material level. In essence, IPC-1752 was able to address many of the original stakeholder concerns.

While the explicitness of IPC-1752 addressed many of the information requirement issues created by RoHS, the utility of IPC-1752 utility is limited to material declaration. FACTS aims to provide a holistic approach to address not only declaration, but also implementation, conformance, and compliance. The application of FACTS will provide us with a mechanism to not only employ IPC-1752 as a RoHS declaration, but also to facilitate conformance and compliance with RoHS. Figure 7 depicts a scenario where FACTS assists a product manufacturer in the US that is interested in having a product (e.g., hair dryer) certified as RoHS-compliant.

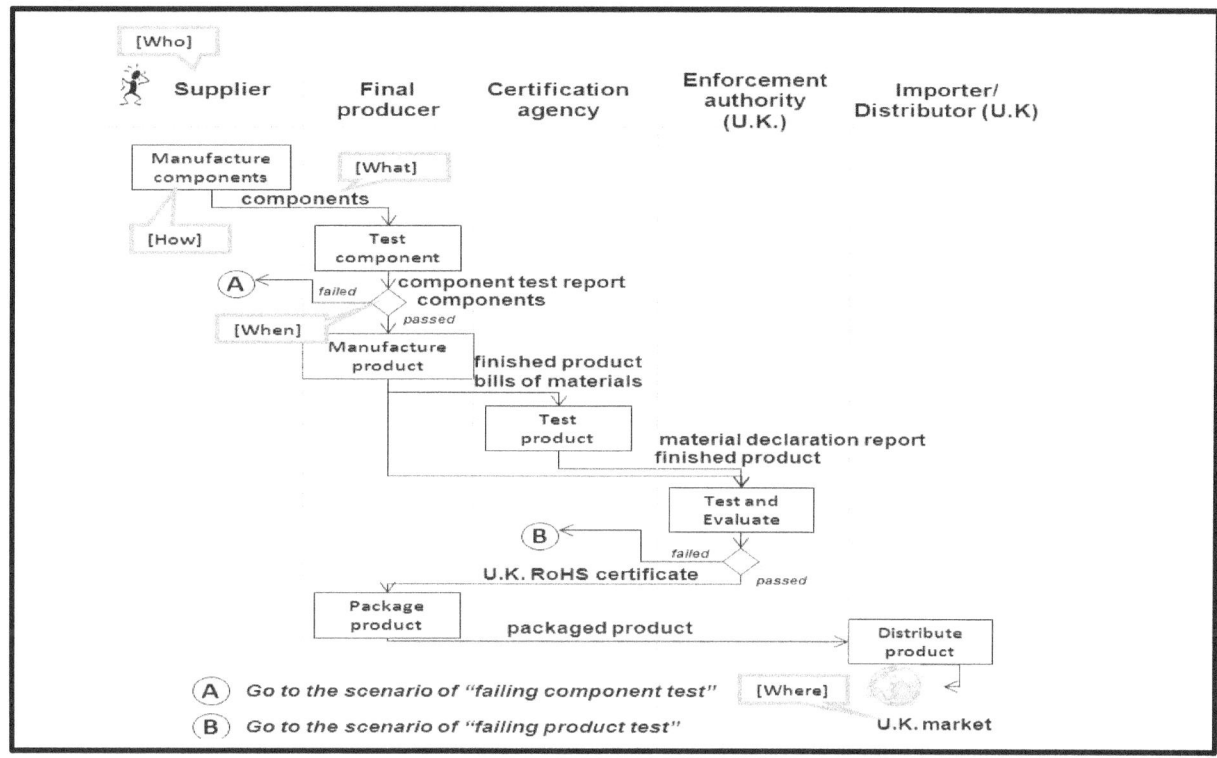

Figure 7. From manufacturing to marketing RoHS-compliant products

Each of the steps in the above scenario were facilitated using FACTS results from the previous sections. The figure details the steps the company may follow to ensure that it is placing a RoHS-compliant product on the market. The individual steps, decisions and processes in Figure 7 are transparent with their respective cells of the Zachman framework. For instance, the component types in this scenario are identified in the conceptual and contextual layers (rows 1 and 2) of the 'what' column in the framework. The types of manufacturing processes for these components is given by the conceptual layer (row 1) of the 'how' column of the framework. The manufacturing processes that affect RoHS compliance are described by the logical and physical layers (rows 3 and 4) of the 'how' column of the framework. The time point of the component test is given by the 'when' column of the framework. Having performed the detailed technical analysis of RoHS using the Zachman framework, we have now integrated the models to describe a business scenario, in complete detail, that will lead to RoHS compliance.

7 Summary

Standards play diverse roles in serving the industry, government and various stakeholders alike. Despite their importance, just like any other endeavor, standards are susceptible to failure. Many standards perish before publication, for various reasons such as technical challenges or failure to achieve consensus. Among published standards, many do not enjoy widespread adoption, often partially due to lack of supporting tools and information infrastructure. We believe significant advances can be made in standards development and adoption. As such, we have developed a methodology that facilitates the conception, deployment and testing of standards.

In this paper, we proposed the Framework for Analysis, Comparison and Testing of Standards -FACTS. FACTS leverages the Zachman framework to analyze standards by separating concerns along orthogonal dimensions. The FACTS analysis of standards occurs at two levels: the stakeholder analysis that identifies stakeholder concerns, and the technical analysis that analyzes the information content of standards at various levels of abstraction. The FACTS facilitates the comparison of analyzed standards and helps identify the gaps and overlaps between them. The comparison methodology provides guidance for the selection of appropriate standards and assists in discovering avenues for standard improvement. FACTS enables two types of testing for standards. FACTS provides guidance for conformance assessment and product compliance with the standard, and a methodology for assessing a standard's scope and consistency within.

FACTS is a first step towards formalizing the way in which standards are conceptualized, developed, and tested. We envision a Computer Aided Standards Development tool based on the FACTS methodology, similar to computer aided development tools in other domains such as software and engineering. We believe that FACTS promotes the development of high quality standards for different applications, thus improving the quality of the applications themselves.

Reference

1. *Standards.gov, What are Standards? 2011.*

2. *Cargill, C.F., Why Standardization Efforts Fail. The Journal of Electronic Publishing, 2011, **14**, DOI: http://dx.doi.org/10.3998/3336451.0014.103.*

3. *Zachman, J.A., A Framework for Information Systems Architecture, IBM Systems Journal, 1999, **38**(2): p. 454.*

4. *Commission, I.E. and T.M. Egyedi, The Life Cycle of Standards, in The Importance of Standards (IEC Lecture series II), 2007.*

5. *Cargill, C.F., Open Systems Standardization-A Business Approach, 1997, Prentice Hall, NY, NY.*

6. *Egyedi, T.M. and K. Blind, The Dynamics of Standards, December 30, 2008, Edward Elgar Publishing.*

7. *Krislov, S., How nations choose product standards and standards change nation, 1997, University of Pittsburgh Press, Pittsburgh, PA.*

8. *Kahin, B. and J. Abbate, eds. Standards Policy for Information Infrastructure, 1995, MIT press, Boston, MA.*

9. *Chopra, A.K. and M.P. Singh, Producing compliant interactions: Conformance, coverage, and interoperability, in Declarative Agent Languages and Technologies IV, 2006, Springer, p. 1-15.*

10. *Witherell, P., et al., An Approach for Identifying Gaps and Overlaps in Standards to Determine Product Applicability, in ASME 2011 IDETC/CIE Conferences, 2011.*

11. *Terzi, S., Elements of product lifecycle management: Definitions, open issues and reference models, 2005, France: Politecnico di Milano, Italy and Henri Poincarre University of Nancy.*

12. *Iyer, R. and T. Gulledge, Product lifecycle management for the US Army weapon systems acquisition, in PLM: Emerging solutions and challenges for global networked enterprise, 2005, Inderscience Publishers.*

13. *Lubell, J., et al., STEP, XML, and UML: Complementary Technologies, ASME Conference Proceedings, 2004,(46970): p. 915-923.*

14. *Allen, R.H. and R.D. Sriram, The Role of Standards in Innovation, Technological Forecasting and Social Change, 2000, 64(2–3): p. 171-181.*

15. *Rachuri, S., et al., Information sharing and exchange in the context of product lifecycle management: Role of standards. Computer-Aided Design, 2008, 40(7): p. 789-800.*

16. *Fiorentini, X., et al., Towards a method for harmonizing information standards, in Proceedings of the fifth annual IEEE international conference on Automation science and engineering, 2009, IEEE Press: Bangalore, India: p. 466-471.*

17. *Panetto, H., S. Baïna, and G. Morel, Mapping the IEC 62264 models onto the Zachman framework for analysing products information traceability: a case study. Journal of Intelligent Manufacturing, 2007, 18: p. 679-698.*

18. *IEC, IEC 62264 -Enterprise-control system integration, 2004.*

19. *Zachman Framework for Heathercare Informatics Standards, University of California Irvine, Editor, 2010, https://apps.adcom.uci.edu/EnterpriseArch/Zachman/Resources/ExampleHealthCareZachman.pdf*

20. *Patient-Provider Secure Messaging Interoperability Specification, HITSP, Editor, 2011, http://www.hitsp.org/ConstructSet_Details.aspx?&PrefixAlpha=1&PrefixNumeric=12.*

21. *Ameta, G. and P. Sarkar, Comparison of Electronics Products Standards for Sustainability, International Jounal for Product Design, 2010, 1(1).*

22. *Sowa, J.F. and J.A. Zachman, Extending and Formalizing the Framework for Information Systems Architecture. IBM Systems Journal, 1992, 31(3).*

23. *Zachman, J.A., John Zachman's Concise Definition of The Zachman Framework, 2011, http://www.zachman.com/about-the-zachman-framework.*

24. *Rachuri, S., et al. Towards a Methodology for Analyzing Sustainability Standards, in The 18th CIRP International Conference of Life Cycle Engineering, 2011, Braunschweig, Germany.*

25. *ISO/IEC 17000, Conformity assessment -- Vocabulary and general principles, 2004.*

26. *Environmental Protection: The Restriction of the Use of Certain Hazardous Substances in Electrical and Electronic Equipment Regulations 2008, E. Parliament, Editor, 2008.*

27. *IPC-1752A – Materials Declaration Management. Available from: www.ipc.org*

28. *Messina, J.V. and E. Simon. Managing Materials Information in the Supply Chain. in The Eighth International Conference on EcoBalance, 2008, Tokyo, Japan.*

29. *The SCRIBA Tool. Software and Systems Division National Institute of Standards and Technology , http://www.nist.gov/itl/ssd/ei/scriba.cfm.*

30. *National Institute of Standards and Technology, Sustainability Standards Portal, 2011, http://www.nist.gov/el/msid/ssp_portal.cfm.*

31. *Waste Electrical Electronic Equipment Directive: Directive 2002/96/EC of the European Parliament and of the council of 27 January 2003 on waste electrical and electronic equipment (WEEE). Official Journal of the European Union, 2003. L 37: p. 24-38.*

32. *Ieee, P., IEEE P1680.1 Standard for Environmental Assessment of Personal Computer Products, Including Notebook Personal Computers, Desktop Personal Computers, and Personal Computer Displays, 2010.*

Appendix. Technical analysis examples for RoHS

This appendix shows information model examples for RoHS, which are analyzed according to the FACTS methodology. The examples only for the first two rows are provided in this appendix. Each example includes meta-models, guidelines of Zachman framework, and explanations to build information model examples.

Row 1. Contextual models

Row 1, What: List of things important to the business	
Zachman guideline	• simply a list of things • a list of common nouns • high level of aggregation
Meta Model	
Explanation	This block contains a list of high level things (nouns) related to a standard. The nouns can be found from standard descriptions such as homepage and technical documents. If a noun means a process, organization, schedule, or location, it should be defined in the column of How, Who, When, or Where, respectively.
Example	Product Bills of Materials Assembly RoHS product category High risk materials Homogeneous material Test reports Certificates of conformance Material declaration RoHS regulation Final producer (Who) Supplier (Who) Market (Where) Manufacturing processes (How) Documentation processes (How)

Row 1, How : List of processes the business performs	
Zachman guideline	• List of processes that the enterprise performs • List of verbs • Relate other lists in Row 1 • Relate existing applications
Meta Model	Verb
Explanation	This block asks for a list of verbs that represent processes in the enterprise platforms. In filling out the "How" block, the processes used to execute the timing cycles in the "When" blocks were considered.
Example	Record, Assemble, Certify, Produce, Enforce, Produce, Sell, Certify, Request, Test, Provide

Row 1, Where: List of locations	
Zachman guideline	• Universe of discourse relative to locations • Proper nouns, names of locations • Defines scope or boundaries of Rows 2 - 5
Meta Model	
Explanation	This cell contains the list of locations where a standard is relevant. It indicates that if a business is interested in working in these regions, it must be concerned about the standard.
Example	

Row 1, Who: List of important organizations	
Zachman guideline	• List of organizations from which the enterprise accepts works
Meta Model	Organization
Explanation	This block provides a list of organizations that are related to the main organization and contribute to the development of the output (product) that needs to be RoHS compliant.
Example	_(illegible faded text)_

Row 1, When: List of events significant to the business	
Zachman guideline	• Records kept at Enterprise level • Gerunds (Commit, Order, etc.) • Each event initiates a cycle (Order-Acquisition cycle) • Relate other lists in Row 1 as well as 'when' Row 6 • As seen by a Dynamics Engineer
Meta Model	_(illegible faded text)_
Explanation	This block provides a list of gerunds or events that initiate cycles. As we are interested in a standard, only standard-applicable events are relevant. For instance, though material extraction may involve hazardous substances, RoHS is not considered until these materials become part of a component. We consider events, which may require testing or reporting for RoHS. These events were categorized in terms of the SCOR chain consisting of source, make, and deliver.
Example	_(illegible faded text)_

Row 1, Why: List of goals	
Zachman guideline	• High level goals • Indefinite, not measurable, long term in nature
Meta Model	
Explanation	This block contains a list of high level goals related to a standard. These are the social, economic and environmental motivations for the creation of, enforcement of, and compliance with the standard.
Example	

Row 2. Business models

Row 2, What : Semantic model	
Zachman guideline	<ul><li>A structural model of "Business Entities" and their relationships</li><li>Serial numbers on the instances of the Things</li><li>Entity/Relationship-type model</li></ul>
Meta Model	
Explanation	The semantic model describes relationships among business entities. Processes, organizations, locations, or events can also be included in the semantic model as business entities, but they should have a tag to indicate which column they belong to in the Zachman framework.
Example	

Row 2, How: Conceptual business process model	
Zachman guideline	<ul><li>Input –process – output model</li><li>Structured model of business processes that the enterprise performs</li><li>Expressing the business transformations that convert raw materials and energy to finished goods and services</li></ul>
Meta Model	
Explanation	This block provides a diagram of how raw "materials" can become finished "goods" based on procedures used. Here the "materials" are RoHS-related inputs, and the "goods" are RoHS-related outputs. The boxes are business processes that represent the transformation procedure, or how, between the two.
Example	

Row 2, Where: Conceptual logistics network	

Zachman guideline	• Linkages imply movement of three categories of things:
	   ○ physical goods
	   ○ information/data
	   ○ money
	• Locations of: Things from Column 1, Processes from Column 2 and People from Column 4

Meta Model	
Explanation	This block provides an information model describing the geographical network of businesses and their markets. The nodes indicate the locations of Manufacturers and Suppliers, and their geographical market regions. The linkages indicate flow of goods and information. The information model provides the RoHS requirement for the different linkages.
Example	

Row 2, Who: Work flow model	
Zachman guideline	<ul><li>A structural model of "Business Entities" and their relationships</li><li>Serial numbers on the instances of the Things</li><li>Entity/Relationship-type model</li></ul>
Meta Model	
Explanation	This block provides the relationships that exist among different entities.
Example	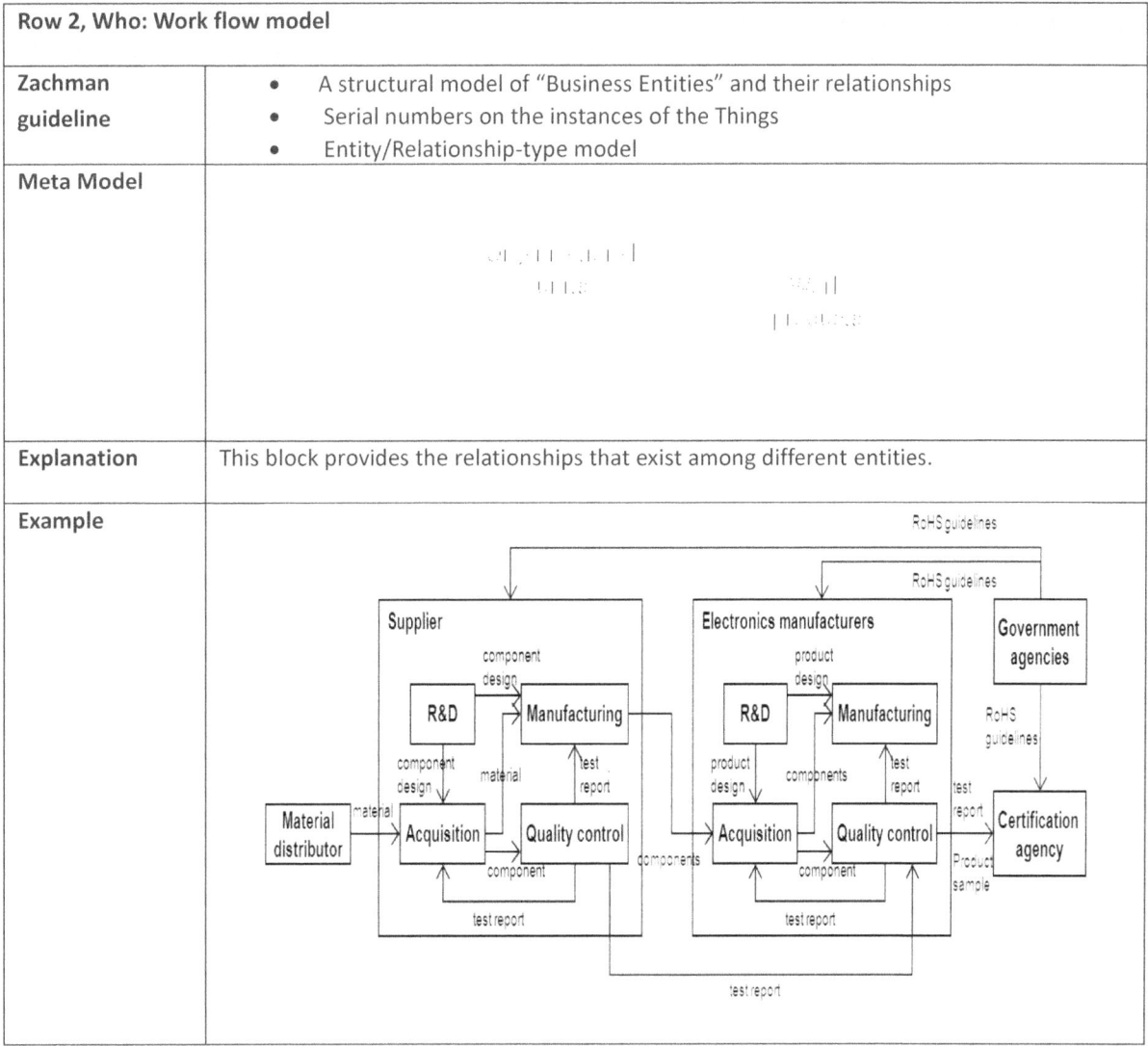

Row 2, When: Conceptual master schedule	
Zachman guideline	• Dynamics model of events-cycles-events • Master schedule for enterprise • Helpful for understanding the interrelationships between cycles
Meta Model	
Explanation	Unlike the last block, which was a list of gerunds, this block is an information model, providing a "master schedule" for when RoHS applies to a product during a cycle and where cycles may overlap. Here we break it up into three models: Source, Make, and Deliver.
Example	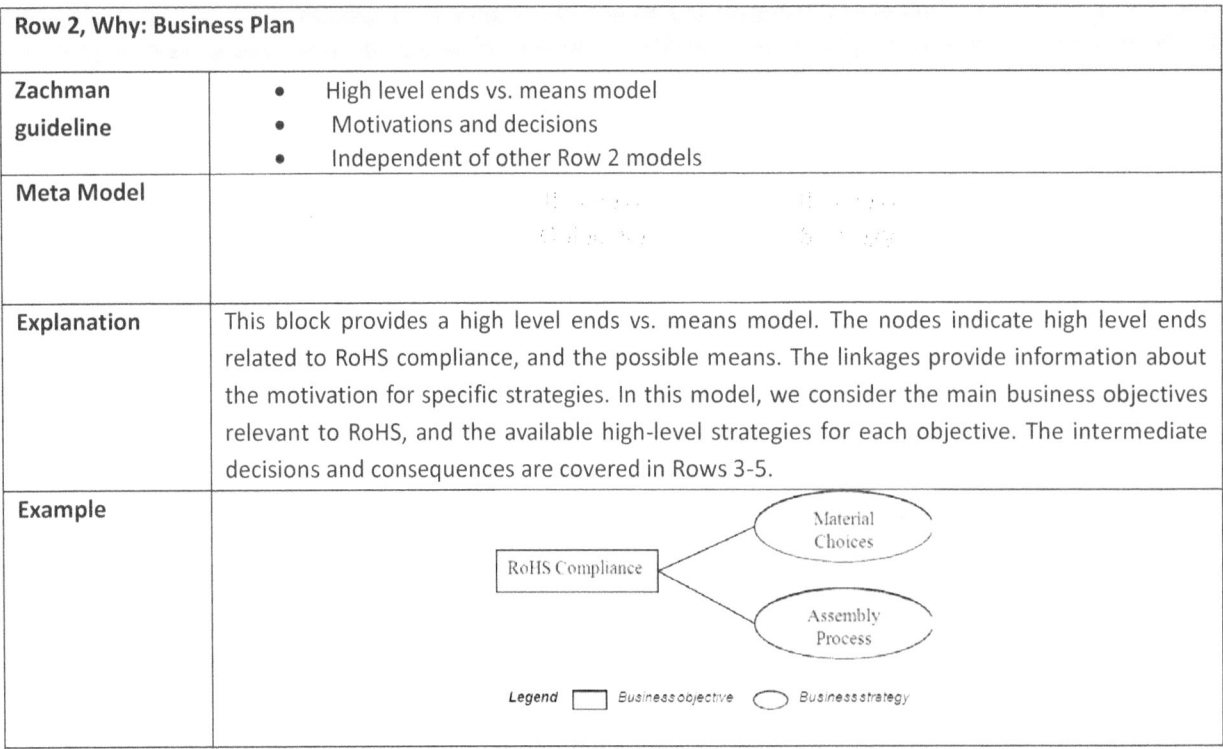

Row 2, Why: Business Plan	
Zachman guideline	• High level ends vs. means model • Motivations and decisions • Independent of other Row 2 models
Meta Model	
Explanation	This block provides a high level ends vs. means model. The nodes indicate high level ends related to RoHS compliance, and the possible means. The linkages provide information about the motivation for specific strategies. In this model, we consider the main business objectives relevant to RoHS, and the available high-level strategies for each objective. The intermediate decisions and consequences are covered in Rows 3-5.
Example	

www.ingramcontent.com/pod-product-compliance
Lightning Source LLC
Chambersburg PA
CBHW080738290526
45790CB00008B/3247